Deep Breathing is my Blanket

an Ami the Llama story

by

Oshri Liron Hakak

BUTTERFLYON BOOKS

First Edition
Copyright © 2023 by Oshri Liron Hakak
All Rights Reserved

Deep Breathing is My Blanket: an Ami the Llama Story
Written and illustrated by Oshri Liron Hakak

Published by Butterflyon Books
Los Angeles
ISBN: 979-8-9868755-7-6

For anyone who needs a blanket.

Ami looked up at the mountain.
The tree called out to her, "Come to me!"
The tree was her friend, so she did.

She sat by the tree and the tree gave her air and taught her to breathe slowly and deeply.

The tree also taught Ami a song:

Deep breathing is my blanket,
And kindness my cocoon.
My deep breath weaves a magic thread
Through life's mysterious loom.

She thanked the tree for the lesson and she gave the tree a hug.

When Ami came down from the mountain, she tested what the tree taught her.

She found that she could use her slow, deep breathing to create threads...

...threads that connect.

Weaving the threads together, she made patches. She then connected the patches with one another.

She saw that her deep breathing was deep weaving.

She kept breathing slowly and deeply and she made herself a scarf to keep warm.

Ami was very grateful for her scarf.
It made her feel safe and cozy.

Feeling safe and cozy,
she got the courage to reach for her goals.

And she got the courage to rest and to be thankful for her life, too.

She decided to keep on deeply breathing, and to keep on deeply weaving, until her scarf...

...became a blanket.
And she remembered...

*Deep breathing is my blanket,
And kindness my cocoon.
My deep breath weaves a magic thread
Through life's mysterious loom.*

With her blanket, Ami felt even more courage. She had so much courage, she could appreciate beauty she hadn't ever let herself notice before.

And she had enough courage to feel certain feelings more than she ever had before... like compassion, the ability to deeply feel what it's like to be in someone else's fur, and also care a lot for them.

Then she saw her friend, Ama, who had no blanket. Ami and Ama had shared an argument some days before.

Now Ami offered to share her blanket with Ama.

Sharing the blanket together,
Ami listened to Ama with deep care,
more than ever before.

Then Ama listened to Ami with the same deep care, more than ever before.

Ami and Ama learned from one another, and they became even better friends.

Then Ami taught Ama a song...

Deep breathing is my blanket,
And kindness my cocoon.
My deep breath weaves a magic thread
Through life's mysterious loom.

Weaving Your Blanket

Try this:

Sit in a relaxed position. Close your eyes and breathe slowly and deeply. Imagine that with every breath you take, you are weaving your own blanket around you. Imagine being in your blanket— calm, safe, and cozy.

Affirmations:

I use my slow, deep breathing to help myself feel safe and calm.

I use my slow, deep breathing to help others feel safe and calm when I listen to them.

I use my slow, deep breathing to weave threads of connection and care within myself.

I use my slow, deep breathing to weave threads of connection and care with others.

Questions:

How does cuddling in a big blanket make me feel?

What are some other ways we can use our slow, deep breathing?

What situations can your slow, deep breathing help you with?

How Did Ami the Llama Come to Be?

Ami the Lama was inspired by Oshri's work with NAMI Westside Los Angeles. NAMI Westside Los Angeles is part of NAMI, a national grassroots mental health advocacy organization that offers free programming and support for people struggling with challenges in their mental health, as well as for those who are supporting loved ones who are going through mental health challenges. The llama has long been an unofficial mascot of NAMI, as the remarkable creatures are living representations of empathy, compassion and strength. You can find out more about NAMI and its offerings at NAMIWLA.org.

As for the name itself, Ami means friend, and we all need friends with great capacity for empathy, compassion and strength. So it was a perfect fit. Ami and NAMI are your friends. You are not alone.

About Oshri

Oshri Hakak is an artist, author, and meditation teacher. His books touch on mental health and mindfulness, and how we can use breath practices and creativity to work with tough emotions. He often blends mindfulness with opening up and exploring creative outlets, encouraging people to use their own voices for their personal healing, and for the well-being of their communities. You can find his daily art on Instagram (@oshrihakak) and more of his books on ButterflyonBooks.com .